# Bread Machine Mastery Cookbook

SARA GARTEN

# TABLE OF CONTENTS

## BONUS BREADS FROM AROUND THE WORLD – EUROPEAN BREAD RECIPES............................................................................................. 125

## BONUS AMERICAN HOLIDAY BREAD RECIPES ............................ 135

# Introduction: Ultimate Bread Machine Cookbook

There's a kind of magic that happens when you combine basic ingredients like flour, water, yeast, and a bit of time. This magical process, known as baking, has been an integral part of human culture for centuries. It's hard to pinpoint when the first bread was made, but one thing is certain: its aroma, taste, and the comfort it brings have made it a staple in households across the globe.

Enter the bread machine, a modern invention that has rekindled the love for homemade bread in countless homes. While purists might argue about the authenticity of machine-made bread versus handcrafted loaves, there's no denying the convenience and consistency a bread machine offers, especially in our fast-paced lives.

In "Bread Machine Cookbook" we'll journey through the wondrous world of bread making, but with a special twist. This guide is tailored specifically for those who own or are interested in owning a bread machine. We aim to demystify the process, offering tips, techniques, and tantalizing recipes to ensure that your bread-making endeavors are successful and, most importantly, delicious.

Whether you're a novice baker just starting out or a seasoned pro looking for some new recipes to try, this book promises a bounty of knowledge and flavors. From understanding the intricacies of the machine to exploring bread from various cultures, we've curated a comprehensive guide for every bread enthusiast.

# The Renaissance of the Bread Machine: A History

The bread machine, a seemingly modern marvel, actually has roots that trace back several decades. In the late 1980s and early 1990s, it was hailed as a revolutionary kitchen gadget. Families flocked to stores, eager to own a machine that promised freshly baked bread with minimal effort.

But how did this fascinating invention come into being?

In 1986, the Japanese company Matsushita Electric Industrial Co., Ltd., known as Panasonic today, introduced the first bread-making machine. The Japanese market, always quick to embrace novel technologies, welcomed it with open arms. The ease of throwing in ingredients and getting a perfect loaf a few hours later was an offer too tempting to refuse.

The success in Japan quickly caught the attention of western markets. Brands like West Bend, Zojirushi, and Breadman started producing their versions, each with unique features and functions. As with any trend, there were skeptics. Traditional bakers viewed it as a compromise on authenticity, while some critics felt the bread lacked the charm and character of hand-made loaves. However, the convenience it offered made it popular among many households.

But as with all trends, the hype around bread machines started to wane by the early 2000s. The advent of artisanal bakeries and the appreciation for handcrafted goods meant that bread machines were often relegated to the back of kitchen cabinets, collecting dust.

However, the story doesn't end there. With the rise of home cooking and DIY trends, the bread machine saw a resurgence. People began to appreciate the machine for what it truly was - not a replacement for traditional baking, but an aid for those who wanted to enjoy homemade bread without the intensive labor.

Today, the bread machine stands as a testament to human ingenuity and the enduring love for bread. Its history is not just a story of an appliance but a reflection of society's changing relationship with food and cooking.

In the subsequent chapters, we will dive deeper into mastering the bread machine, from understanding its mechanics to exploring global bread recipes. But as we move forward, it's essential to remember the rich history and evolution that brought this marvel to our kitchens.

# Ingredients 101: Understanding the Basics

For every loaf of bread that emerges golden and fragrant from the oven, there's a careful selection of ingredients that went into its creation. Understanding these basics is akin to knowing the letters of an alphabet before crafting a story. Let's dive deep into the fundamental components of bread-making, unraveling the mysteries and roles of each ingredient.

## Flour: The Backbone

Every building needs a strong foundation, and for bread, it's the flour. But not all flours are created equal.

1. **Wheat Flour:** The most common type used in bread-making due to its gluten-forming properties. Depending on the milling process and the part of the wheat grain used, we get different varieties:
   - **Whole Wheat Flour:** Uses the entire grain, rich in fiber, and has a nutty taste.
   - **Bread Flour:** High in gluten, it's perfect for yeasty breads that need good structure.
   - **All-Purpose Flour:** A versatile option suitable for a range of baked goods.
   - **Cake or Pastry Flour:** Low in gluten and perfect for softer baked goods.

2. **Non-Wheat Flours:** Flours like rye, barley, and oat, which have different gluten levels and properties. Often mixed with wheat flour to ensure structure.

## Water: The Activator

Might seem mundane, but water plays multiple roles:

1. **Hydration:** It hydrates the proteins in the flour to form gluten.
2. **Activation:** It activates the yeast, allowing it to feed on the sugars and produce carbon dioxide.
3. **Temperature Control:** The temperature of water can influence dough temperature, impacting yeast activity.

## Yeast: The Leavener

This tiny organism is what breathes life into the dough. Consuming sugars, it releases carbon dioxide, causing the dough to rise.

1. **Active Dry Yeast:** Needs activation in warm water before use.
2. **Instant Yeast:** Can be mixed directly with flour, preferred for its potency and reliability.
3. **Fresh Yeast:** A soft, crumbly block used traditionally, but with a short shelf life.

## Salt: The Flavor Enhancer

While it adds flavor, salt also controls yeast activity, preventing over-fermentation, and strengthens the gluten network.

## Fats: For Softness and Flavor

Butter, oils, and lard not only impart taste but also influence the bread's crumb and texture. They can tenderize the loaf, making it softer.

## Sugars and Sweeteners: Food for Yeast

Beyond sweetness, sugars provide food for yeast and contribute to the browning of the crust. From granulated sugar, honey, molasses to malt, the choice affects both flavor and color.

## Eggs and Dairy: Richness and Structure

Eggs add structure, moisture, and richness, while milk tenderizes the bread, offering a softer crumb and a golden crust.

## Add-Ins: Diversity in Every Bite

From nuts, seeds, dried fruits to herbs and spices, these ingredients can turn a simple loaf into a gourmet experience.

## Conclusion

While the list of potential ingredients in bread-making is vast, understanding these fundamentals allows you to approach every recipe with knowledge and confidence. Each ingredient, in its way, contributes to the flavor, structure, and texture of the bread. Like an orchestra where each instrument plays its part, in bread-making, every ingredient has its role in the symphony of flavors and aromas.

# The Art and Science of Fermentation – Unlocking Flavors

One of the most captivating aspects of bread-making is fermentation. It's not just a simple process, but a transformative journey that each grain of flour undergoes, orchestrated by the seemingly mundane yeast. Fermentation is where the true magic of bread-making lies.

You see, fermentation is a process where the carbohydrates in the dough are broken down by yeast and bacteria into carbon dioxide and alcohols. This not only helps the bread rise, but it also imparts distinct flavors that set apart a freshly baked loaf from a store-bought one.

In traditional bread-making, time was the essential ingredient. Bakers would let their dough ferment for hours, sometimes even days, allowing the slow process of fermentation to develop complex flavors in the bread. The result? A loaf with a crisp crust, a tender crumb, and a flavor profile that was both tangy and deeply aromatic.

But how does this work in a bread machine, you might wonder? The beauty of modern bread machines lies in their ability to recreate this age-old process in a fraction of the time, without compromising on quality. Most machines come with a fermentation or 'proofing' setting, which provides the dough with the optimal temperature and environment for the yeast to work its magic.

Temperature plays a crucial role in fermentation. A warmer environment accelerates the activity of the yeast, leading to a faster rise. However, a slower fermentation at a cooler temperature often results in a bread with better texture and more nuanced flavors. This is the reason behind the revered "cold fermentation" method used in many artisanal bakeries, where the dough is allowed to ferment in a refrigerator for an extended period.

Apart from the yeast, there's another player in the game: lactic acid bacteria. Found naturally in the environment and even on the surface of grains, these bacteria contribute to the tangy flavor found in sourdough breads. They work in tandem with yeast, creating a diverse ecosystem within your dough, leading to a loaf that's not just delicious but also unique.

To master the art of fermentation is to understand that patience often yields the best results. It's about recognizing that bread-making is as much a science as it is an art. Each loaf tells a story of transformation, a testament to the wonders of nature, and the beauty of time.

# BONUS Vegan Ventures: Dairy-free, Egg-free Marvels

Veganism, once a niche lifestyle, has become a widespread movement, emphasizing the importance of animal welfare and environmental sustainability. While vegan choices have proliferated across culinary avenues, bread-making remains a domain where dairy and eggs often make an appearance. However, the beauty of bread-making is its adaptability. With a few crafty substitutions and a pinch of innovation, you can produce vegan bread that's every bit as delicious as its traditional counterpart. This chapter shines a light on vegan bread-making, ensuring that no one has to compromise on taste or ethics.

## The Role of Dairy and Eggs in Bread

Before diving into vegan substitutes, it's essential to understand the roles dairy and eggs play in bread:

1. **Dairy:** Milk and butter primarily enhance the bread's flavor, texture, and shelf life. They can make bread softer, richer, and extend its freshness.
2. **Eggs:** Often used in enriched bread, eggs contribute to the bread's structure, moisture, color, and flavor.

## Crafty Vegan Substitutes

Achieving that perfect loaf without dairy or eggs is entirely feasible with these ingenious swaps:

1. **Milk Alternatives:** There's a plethora of plant-based milk available today. Almond, soy, oat, rice, and coconut milk can seamlessly replace cow's milk in recipes. Each brings its unique flavor and texture, so experimenting can lead to delightful discoveries.
2. **Butter Replacements:** Coconut oil is a popular substitute, providing a similar fat content without the dairy. Vegan margarine is another option, closely mimicking the flavor and texture of butter. For a more rustic touch, olive oil can be used in some bread recipes.
3. **Egg Alternatives:** Eggs can be a bit trickier to replace, but numerous solutions exist:
   - **Flaxseed or Chia 'Eggs':** When mixed with water, ground flaxseed or chia seeds form a gelatinous mixture, mirroring the binding properties of eggs.
   - **Applesauce:** This not only replaces the moisture from eggs but also adds a hint of sweetness.
   - **Silken Tofu:** When blended, it can mimic the consistency of beaten eggs, making it suitable for denser bread like banana bread or zucchini bread.
   - **Vinegar and Baking Powder:** In combination, these can create a leavening effect similar to that of eggs.

## Baking Vegan Bread: Tips and Tricks

1. **Pay Attention to Hydration:** Some vegan substitutes can alter the hydration levels of your dough. For instance, while coconut milk is creamy and rich, almond milk might be more watery. Adjust your recipe accordingly.
2. **Temperature Matters:** Plant-based fats like coconut oil have different melting points than butter. Be mindful of this when proofing your dough, especially if using a warm environment.
3. **Experiment with Flavors:** Vegan bread-making offers a chance to get creative. Incorporate nuts, seeds, dried fruits, or even vegan chocolate chips for a delightful twist.

# RECIPIES

# BASIC BREAD RECIPES

## Basic White Bread

*Ingredients:*

- 500 gr bread flour
- 300 ml warm water
- 2 teaspoons active dry yeast
- 10 gr salt
- 15 gr sugar
- 25 gr unsalted butter, softened

*Instructions:*

1. Add water, sugar, and yeast to the bread machine pan. Allow it to sit for 10 minutes.
2. Add flour, salt, and butter.
3. Set the machine to the basic bread setting and start.

# Whole Wheat Bread

*Ingredients:*

- 400 gr whole wheat flour
- 100 gr bread flour
- 320 ml warm water
- 2 teaspoons active dry yeast
- 10 gr salt
- 25 gr honey
- 25 gr unsalted butter

*Instructions:*

1. Add water, honey, and yeast to the bread machine pan. Wait for 10 minutes.
2. Add flours, salt, and butter.
3. Choose the whole wheat setting on your machine and start.

# French Bread

*Ingredients:*

- 500 gr bread flour
- 290 ml warm water
- 2 teaspoons active dry yeast
- 10 gr salt
- 10 gr sugar

*Instructions:*

1. Add water, sugar, and yeast to the bread machine pan. Let sit for 10 minutes.
2. Add flour and salt.
3. Choose the French bread setting on your machine and start.

## Multi-grain Bread

*Ingredients:*

- 250 gr bread flour
- 100 gr whole wheat flour
- 50 gr oats
- 50 gr rye flour
- 50 gr cornmeal
- 320 ml warm water
- 2 teaspoons active dry yeast
- 15 gr salt
- 25 gr honey
- 25 gr unsalted butter

*Instructions:*

1. Add water, honey, and yeast to the bread machine pan. Wait for 10 minutes.
2. Add all flours, oats, cornmeal, salt, and butter.
3. Set the machine to the whole wheat or multi-grain setting and start.

# Rye Bread

*Ingredients:*

- 350 gr bread flour
- 150 gr rye flour
- 300 ml warm water
- 2 teaspoons active dry yeast
- 15 gr salt
- 20 gr sugar
- 20 gr unsalted butter

*Instructions:*

1. Add water, sugar, and yeast to the bread machine pan. Wait for 10 minutes.
2. Add flours, salt, and butter.
3. Choose the basic bread setting and start.

# Oat Bread

*Ingredients:*

- 400 gr bread flour
- 100 gr oats
- 300 ml warm milk
- 2 teaspoons active dry yeast
- 10 gr salt
- 25 gr honey
- 20 gr unsalted butter

*Instructions:*

1. Add milk, honey, and yeast to the bread machine pan. Wait for 10 minutes.
2. Add flour, oats, salt, and butter.
3. Choose the basic bread setting and start.

# Italian Herb Bread

*Ingredients:*

- 500 gr bread flour
- 300 ml warm water
- 2 teaspoons active dry yeast
- 10 gr salt
- 10 gr sugar
- 1 tablespoon Italian seasoning (a mix of oregano, basil, rosemary, etc.)

*Instructions:*

1. Add water, sugar, and yeast to the bread machine pan. Wait for 10 minutes.
2. Add flour, salt, and Italian seasoning.
3. Choose the basic bread setting and start.

# Cinnamon Raisin Bread

*Ingredients:*

- 500 gr bread flour
- 320 ml warm water
- 2 teaspoons active dry yeast
- 10 gr salt
- 50 gr sugar
- 2 teaspoons cinnamon
- 150 gr raisins

*Instructions:*

1. Add water, sugar, and yeast to the bread machine pan. Wait for 10 minutes.
2. Add flour, salt, cinnamon, and raisins.
3. Choose the fruit/nut setting or basic bread setting and start.

**General Tip for All Recipes:** Ensure all ingredients, especially liquids and yeast, are at room temperature unless stated otherwise. This encourages the yeast to work effectively, leading to a better rise and overall bread texture.

# SPICE, HERB, AND VEGETABLE BREADS RECIPES

## Rosemary Olive Bread

*Ingredients:*

- 250 ml warm water
- 30 ml olive oil
- 375 g bread flour
- 5 g salt
- 2 tablespoons fresh rosemary, chopped
- 50 g pitted olives, chopped
- 2 1/2 teaspoons bread machine yeast

*Method:*

1. Add the warm water and olive oil to the bread machine pan.
2. Add the flour, ensuring it covers the liquid.
3. Make a well in the center and add the yeast.
4. Place salt, rosemary, and olives around the flour.
5. Set the machine on the "Basic Bread" setting and start.
6. Once baked, cool on a wire rack.

# Turmeric and Cumin Loaf

*Ingredients:*

- 260 ml warm water
- 375 g bread flour
- 5 g salt
- 5 g ground turmeric
- 3 g ground cumin
- 2 1/2 teaspoons bread machine yeast

*Method:*

1. Pour the warm water into the bread machine pan.
2. Cover with flour, making a well in the center for the yeast.
3. Add salt, turmeric, and cumin around the flour.
4. Choose the "Basic Bread" setting and start.
5. Cool on a wire rack after baking.

# Spinach and Feta Cheese Bread

*Ingredients:*

- 230 ml warm water
- 375 g bread flour
- 5 g salt
- 150 g fresh spinach, chopped
- 100 g feta cheese, crumbled
- 2 1/2 teaspoons bread machine yeast

*Method:*

1. Start with warm water in the bread machine pan.
2. Add flour and create a well in the center for yeast.
3. Add salt, spinach, and feta around the flour.
4. Use the "Basic Bread" setting and start.
5. Once done, cool on a wire rack.

# Garlic and Parsley Bread

*Ingredients:*

- 250 ml warm water
- 30 ml olive oil
- 375 g bread flour
- 5 g salt
- 4 garlic cloves, minced
- 3 tablespoons fresh parsley, chopped
- 2 1/2 teaspoons bread machine yeast

*Method:*

1. Pour warm water and olive oil into the bread machine pan.
2. Cover with flour, making a center well for the yeast.
3. Place salt, garlic, and parsley around the flour.
4. Set the machine on "Basic Bread" and start.
5. Cool on a wire rack post-baking.

# Zucchini Walnut Bread

*Ingredients:*

- 230 ml warm water
- 375 g bread flour
- 5 g salt
- 150 g zucchini, shredded
- 50 g walnuts, chopped
- 2 1/2 teaspoons bread machine yeast

*Method:*

1. Add warm water to the bread machine pan.
2. Add flour, ensuring it covers the liquid, and create a well for yeast.
3. Surround the flour with salt, zucchini, and walnuts.
4. Use the "Basic Bread" setting and begin.
5. Once baked, cool on a wire rack.

# Tomato Basil Bread

*Ingredients:*

- 240 ml warm water
- 375 g bread flour
- 5 g salt
- 100 g sun-dried tomatoes, chopped
- 20 g fresh basil, chopped
- 2 1/2 teaspoons bread machine yeast

*Method:*

1. Pour warm water into the bread machine pan.
2. Cover with flour and make a well for the yeast.
3. Add salt, tomatoes, and basil around the flour.
4. Set the machine to "Basic Bread" and start.
5. Post baking, cool on a wire rack.

# Sweet Potato and Rosemary Bread

*Ingredients:*

- 200 ml warm water
- 100 ml sweet potato puree
- 375 g bread flour
- 5 g salt
- 2 tablespoons fresh rosemary, chopped
- 2 1/2 teaspoons bread machine yeast

*Method:*

1. Add warm water and sweet potato puree to the bread machine pan.
2. Add the flour, making a center well for the yeast.
3. Surround the flour with salt and rosemary.
4. Choose the "Basic Bread" setting and start.
5. Once done, cool on a wire rack.

# Cilantro and Lemon Loaf

*Ingredients:*

- 250 ml warm water
- 375 g bread flour
- 5 g salt
- Zest of 1 lemon
- 20 g fresh cilantro, finely chopped
- 30 ml lemon juice
- 2 1/2 teaspoons bread machine yeast

*Method:*

1. Start with warm water in the bread machine pan.
2. Add flour, ensuring it covers the liquid, and create a well for the yeast.
3. Surround the flour with salt, lemon zest, and cilantro.
4. Squeeze in the lemon juice.
5. Set the machine to "Basic Bread" and start.
6. Once baked, allow to cool on a wire rack.

# Onion and Chive Bread

*Ingredients:*

- 240 ml warm water
- 375 g bread flour
- 5 g salt
- 50 g fresh chives, chopped
- 50 g onion, finely chopped
- 2 1/2 teaspoons bread machine yeast

*Method:*

1. Pour the warm water into the bread machine pan.
2. Add flour, creating a well in the center for the yeast.
3. Add salt, chives, and onion around the flour.
4. Use the "Basic Bread" setting and start.
5. Cool on a wire rack after baking.

# Jalapeño and Cheese Loaf

*Ingredients:*

- 240 ml warm water
- 375 g bread flour
- 5 g salt
- 2 jalapeños, finely diced
- 100 g cheddar cheese, shredded
- 2 1/2 teaspoons bread machine yeast

*Method:*

1. Begin with warm water in the bread machine pan.
2. Add flour and make a well in the center for the yeast.
3. Surround the flour with salt, jalapeños, and cheese.
4. Set the machine to the "Basic Bread" setting and start.
5. Once baked, cool on a wire rack.

# Basil and Pine Nut Bread

*Ingredients:*

- 240 ml warm water
- 375 g bread flour
- 5 g salt
- 20 g fresh basil, chopped
- 50 g pine nuts
- 2 1/2 teaspoons bread machine yeast

*Method:*

1. Start by adding the warm water to the bread machine pan.
2. Layer with flour, creating a well for the yeast.
3. Add salt, basil, and pine nuts around the flour.
4. Choose the "Basic Bread" setting and start.
5. Allow to cool on a wire rack after baking.

# Peppercorn and Olive Oil Loaf

*Ingredients:*

- 240 ml warm water
- 40 ml olive oil
- 375 g bread flour
- 5 g salt
- 5 g crushed black peppercorns
- 2 1/2 teaspoons bread machine yeast

*Method:*

1. Pour warm water and olive oil into the bread machine pan.
2. Add flour, ensuring it covers the liquid, and make a well for the yeast.
3. Surround the flour with salt and crushed peppercorns.
4. Set the machine on the "Basic Bread" setting and start.
5. Cool on a wire rack post-baking.

# Roasted Garlic and Parmesan Bread

*Ingredients:*

- 250 ml warm water
- 375 g bread flour
- 5 g salt
- 1 head of roasted garlic, mashed
- 50 g grated Parmesan cheese
- 2 1/2 teaspoons bread machine yeast

*Method:*

1. Begin with warm water in the bread machine pan.
2. Add flour, creating a center well for yeast.
3. Surround the flour with salt, roasted garlic mash, and Parmesan cheese.
4. Set the machine to "Basic Bread" and start.
5. Once baked, cool on a wire rack.

# Carrot and Thyme Loaf

*Ingredients:*

- 240 ml warm water
- 375 g bread flour
- 5 g salt
- 100 g grated carrot
- 3 g fresh thyme leaves
- 2 1/2 teaspoons bread machine yeast

*Method:*

1. Add the warm water to the bread machine pan.
2. Cover with flour, creating a well in the center for the yeast.
3. Place salt, grated carrot, and thyme leaves around the flour.
4. Set the machine to the "Basic Bread" setting and start.
5. Once done, allow to cool on a wire rack.

# Beet and Fennel Bread

*Ingredients:*

- 240 ml warm water
- 100 g beet puree
- 375 g bread flour
- 5 g salt
- 10 g fennel seeds
- 2 1/2 teaspoons bread machine yeast

*Method:*

1. Begin with warm water and beet puree in the bread machine pan.
2. Layer the flour, ensuring a well in the center for the yeast.
3. Add salt and fennel seeds around the flour.
4. Use the "Basic Bread" setting and start.
5. Once baked, cool on a wire rack.

## Pumpkin and Sage Loaf

*Ingredients:*

- 200 ml warm water
- 100 ml pumpkin puree
- 375 g bread flour
- 5 g salt
- 5 g dried sage or 10 g fresh sage, finely chopped
- 2 1/2 teaspoons bread machine yeast

*Method:*

1. Combine the warm water and pumpkin puree in the bread machine pan.
2. Add flour, making a center well for the yeast.
3. Sprinkle salt and sage around the flour.
4. Set the machine to the "Basic Bread" setting and start.
5. Cool on a wire rack after baking.

# Coriander and Lime Bread

*Ingredients:*

- 240 ml warm water
- 375 g bread flour
- 5 g salt
- Zest of 1 lime
- 5 g ground coriander
- 30 ml lime juice
- 2 1/2 teaspoons bread machine yeast

*Method:*

1. Start with warm water in the bread machine pan.
2. Cover with flour, making a well in the center for the yeast.
3. Add salt, lime zest, and ground coriander around the flour.
4. Squeeze in the lime juice.
5. Choose the "Basic Bread" setting and start.
6. Once done, cool on a wire rack.

# Spinach and Parmesan Bread

*Ingredients:*

- 240 ml warm water
- 375 g bread flour
- 5 g salt
- 150 g fresh spinach, finely chopped
- 50 g grated Parmesan cheese
- 2 1/2 teaspoons bread machine yeast

*Method:*

1. Pour warm water into the bread machine pan.
2. Add flour, creating a well in the center for the yeast.
3. Surround the flour with salt, spinach, and Parmesan cheese.
4. Use the "Basic Bread" setting and begin.
5. After baking, allow to cool on a wire rack.

# Ginger and Spring Onion Bread

*Ingredients:*

- 250 ml warm water
- 375 g bread flour
- 5 g salt
- 20 g fresh ginger, finely grated
- 50 g spring onions, finely chopped
- 2 1/2 teaspoons bread machine yeast

*Method:*

1. Add warm water to the bread machine pan.
2. Layer with flour, creating a well in the center for the yeast.
3. Add salt, ginger, and spring onions around the flour.
4. Set the machine to the "Basic Bread" setting and start.
5. Once baked, cool on a wire rack.

## Dill and Potato Bread

*Ingredients:*

- 240 ml warm water
- 100 g mashed potato (no milk or butter added)
- 375 g bread flour
- 5 g salt
- 10 g fresh dill, finely chopped
- 2 1/2 teaspoons bread machine yeast

*Method:*

1. Start by pouring warm water and mashed potato into the bread machine pan.
2. Add flour, ensuring a well in the center for the yeast.
3. Surround the flour with salt and dill.
4. Use the "Basic Bread" setting and start.
5. Once done, allow to cool on a wire rack.

# Horseradish and Cheddar Bread

*Ingredients:*

- 250 ml warm water
- 375 g bread flour
- 5 g salt
- 30 g prepared horseradish
- 100 g cheddar cheese, shredded
- 2 1/2 teaspoons bread machine yeast

*Method:*

1. Pour warm water into the bread machine pan.
2. Layer with flour, creating a center well for the yeast.
3. Place salt, horseradish, and cheddar around the flour.
4. Set the machine to the "Basic Bread" setting and start.
5. After baking, cool on a wire rack.

# MULTIGRAIN BREAD RECIPES

## Classic Multigrain Bread

*Ingredients:*

- 200 gr bread flour
- 100 gr whole wheat flour
- 50 gr oats
- 50 gr flaxseed meal
- 50 gr sunflower seeds
- 320 ml warm water
- 2 teaspoons active dry yeast
- 10 gr salt
- 25 gr honey

*Instructions:*

1. Add warm water, honey, and yeast to the bread machine pan. Let sit for 10 minutes.
2. Add all flours, oats, flaxseed meal, sunflower seeds, and salt.
3. Select the whole wheat or multigrain setting and start.

*Tip:* Soak sunflower seeds in water for an hour before use to prevent them from drawing moisture from the bread.

# Rye & Barley Bread

*Ingredients:*

- 250 gr bread flour
- 100 gr rye flour
- 100 gr barley flour
- 320 ml warm water
- 2 teaspoons active dry yeast
- 10 gr salt
- 15 gr molasses

*Instructions:*

1. Mix warm water, molasses, and yeast in the bread machine pan. Allow to sit for 10 minutes.
2. Add flours and salt.
3. Use the whole wheat or multigrain setting and start.

*Tip:* Molasses gives a rich color and subtle sweetness that complements the rye and barley flavors.

## Quinoa Power Loaf

*Ingredients:*

- 300 gr bread flour
- 100 gr cooked quinoa
- 50 gr oats
- 50 gr flaxseeds
- 300 ml warm water
- 2 teaspoons active dry yeast
- 10 gr salt
- 20 gr honey

*Instructions:*

1. Mix warm water, honey, and yeast in the bread machine pan. Allow to sit for 10 minutes.
2. Add flour, cooked quinoa, oats, flaxseeds, and salt.
3. Use the basic or whole wheat setting and start.

*Tip:* Toast the quinoa slightly before cooking for a nuttier flavor.

# Seed Lovers' Bread

*Ingredients:*

- 250 gr bread flour
- 100 gr whole wheat flour
- 50 gr sunflower seeds
- 50 gr pumpkin seeds
- 50 gr sesame seeds
- 320 ml warm water
- 2 teaspoons active dry yeast
- 10 gr salt

*Instructions:*

1. Add warm water and yeast to the bread machine pan. Let sit for 10 minutes.
2. Add flours, seeds, and salt.
3. Use the whole wheat or multigrain setting and start.

*Tip:* To enhance the seed flavor, consider lightly toasting them before adding.

# Millet & Oat Bread

*Ingredients:*

- 300 gr bread flour
- 100 gr oats
- 50 gr millet
- 320 ml warm milk
- 2 teaspoons active dry yeast
- 10 gr salt
- 20 gr honey

*Instructions:*

1. Mix warm milk, honey, and yeast in the bread machine pan. Wait 10 minutes.
2. Add flour, oats, millet, and salt.
3. Select the basic or whole wheat setting and start.

*Tip:* Millet offers a slight crunch and a delicate sweetness, complementing the creamy texture of oats.

# Buckwheat & Corn Bread

*Ingredients:*

- 250 gr bread flour
- 100 gr buckwheat flour
- 50 gr cornmeal
- 320 ml warm water
- 2 teaspoons active dry yeast
- 10 gr salt
- 15 gr maple syrup

*Instructions:*

1. Combine warm water, maple syrup, and yeast in the bread machine pan. Let sit for 10 minutes.
2. Add flours and cornmeal, followed by the salt.
3. Use the whole wheat or multigrain setting and start.

*Tip:* Buckwheat flour can make the bread dense; ensure not to add more than recommended.

# Chia & Spelt Loaf

*Ingredients:*

- 250 gr bread flour
- 100 gr spelt flour
- 50 gr chia seeds
- 320 ml warm water
- 2 teaspoons active dry yeast
- 10 gr salt
- 20 gr honey

*Instructions:*

1. Mix warm water, honey, and yeast in the bread machine pan. Allow to sit for 10 minutes.
2. Add flours, chia seeds, and salt.
3. Use the whole wheat or multigrain setting and start.

*Tip:* Chia seeds can absorb a lot of moisture. Ensure your dough is not too dry; if so, add a little more water.

# Brown Rice & Linseed Bread

*Ingredients:*

- 300 gr bread flour
- 100 gr brown rice flour
- 50 gr ground linseeds (flaxseeds)
- 320 ml warm water
- 2 teaspoons active dry yeast
- 10 gr salt

*Instructions:*

1. Combine warm water and yeast in the bread machine pan. Let sit for 10 minutes.
2. Add flours, linseeds, and salt.
3. Select the whole wheat or multigrain setting and start.

*Tip:* Brown rice flour gives a gentle nuttiness, perfectly complemented by the earthy tones of linseed.

# HERB-INFUSED BREAD RECIPES

## Rosemary Olive Bread

*Ingredients:*

- 500 gr bread flour
- 310 ml warm water
- 2 teaspoons active dry yeast
- 10 gr salt
- 2 tablespoons chopped fresh rosemary
- 100 gr pitted and chopped black olives

*Instructions:*

1. Add water and yeast to the bread machine pan. Allow it to sit for 10 minutes.
2. Add flour, salt, rosemary, and olives.
3. Set the machine to the basic bread setting and start.

*Tip:* Fresh rosemary is crucial for a fragrant aroma, but if you must use dried rosemary, reduce the amount by half.

# Basil Parmesan Bread

*Ingredients:*

- 500 gr bread flour
- 300 ml warm milk
- 2 teaspoons active dry yeast
- 10 gr salt
- 3 tablespoons chopped fresh basil
- 100 gr grated Parmesan cheese

*Instructions:*

1. Add milk and yeast to the bread machine pan. Wait for 10 minutes.
2. Add flour, salt, basil, and Parmesan cheese.
3. Choose the basic bread setting and start.

*Tip:* The cheese provides a salty touch, so be careful with any additional salt.

# Garlic Herb Bread

*Ingredients:*

- 500 gr bread flour
- 320 ml warm water
- 2 teaspoons active dry yeast
- 10 gr salt
- 3 garlic cloves, minced
- 1 tablespoon each of chopped fresh parsley, thyme, and rosemary

*Instructions:*

1. Add water, and yeast to the bread machine pan. Wait for 10 minutes.
2. Add flour, salt, garlic, and herbs.
3. Set machine to basic bread setting and start.

*Tip:* To prevent garlic from becoming overpowering, ensure it's finely minced.

# Cilantro Lime Bread

*Ingredients:*

- 500 gr bread flour
- 300 ml warm water
- 2 teaspoons active dry yeast
- 10 gr salt
- 3 tablespoons chopped fresh cilantro
- Zest of 1 lime

*Instructions:*

1. Add water and yeast to the bread machine pan. Allow to sit for 10 minutes.
2. Add flour, salt, cilantro, and lime zest.
3. Choose the basic bread setting and start.

*Tip:* Lime zest adds a burst of freshness; ensure you only zest the green part and avoid the bitter white pith.

# Dill & Onion Bread

*Ingredients:*

- 500 gr bread flour
- 310 ml warm water
- 2 teaspoons active dry yeast
- 10 gr salt
- 3 tablespoons chopped fresh dill
- 50 gr finely chopped onion

*Instructions:*

1. Add water and yeast to the bread machine pan. Wait for 10 minutes.
2. Add flour, salt, dill, and onion.
3. Set the machine to the basic bread setting and start.

*Tip:* Dill has a unique taste; you can adjust the amount based on your preference.

# Oregano Tomato Bread

*Ingredients:*

- 500 gr bread flour
- 320 ml warm water
- 2 teaspoons active dry yeast
- 10 gr salt
- 2 tablespoons chopped fresh oregano
- 100 gr sun-dried tomatoes, chopped

*Instructions:*

1. Add water and yeast to the bread machine pan. Wait for 10 minutes.
2. Add flour, salt, oregano, and sun-dried tomatoes.
3. Choose the basic bread setting and start.

*Tip:* Sun-dried tomatoes in oil can be used, but ensure they are well-drained to avoid excess moisture.

## Sage & Walnut Bread

*Ingredients:*

- 500 gr bread flour
- 300 ml warm milk
- 2 teaspoons active dry yeast
- 10 gr salt
- 2 tablespoons chopped fresh sage
- 100 gr chopped walnuts

*Instructions:*

1. Add milk and yeast to the bread machine pan. Wait for 10 minutes.
2. Add flour, salt, sage, and walnuts.
3. Set machine to basic bread setting and start.

*Tip:* Toasting the walnuts before adding can enhance their nutty flavor.

# Mint & Feta Bread

*Ingredients:*

- 500 gr bread flour
- 310 ml warm water
- 2 teaspoons active dry yeast
- 8 gr salt
- 3 tablespoons chopped fresh mint
- 100 gr crumbled feta cheese

*Instructions:*

1. Add water and yeast to the bread machine pan. Wait for 10 minutes.
2. Add flour, salt, mint, and feta.
3. Choose the basic bread setting and start.

*Tip:* Use a mild feta cheese so that its saltiness doesn't overpower the bread.

**General Tip for All Recipes:** Fresh herbs provide the best flavor. However, if you're using dried herbs, reduce the quantity by one third as they are more concentrated. Always store your bread in a cool, dry place to preserve its freshness.

# DELIGHTFUL BREAKFAST BREAD RECIPES

## Classic Breakfast Loaf

*Ingredients:*

- 300 ml warm water
- 450 g bread flour
- 5 g salt
- 5 g sugar
- 2 1/2 teaspoons bread machine yeast

*Method:*

1. Add warm water to the bread machine pan.
2. Top with flour, sugar, and salt, leaving a well in the center for the yeast.
3. Select the "Basic Bread" setting and start. Once baked, cool on a wire rack.

# Cinnamon Raisin Bread

*Ingredients:*

- 300 ml warm water
- 450 g bread flour
- 5 g salt
- 5 g sugar
- 2 g cinnamon
- 100 g raisins
- 2 1/2 teaspoons bread machine yeast

*Method:*

1. Pour warm water into the pan.
2. Add flour, sugar, salt, and cinnamon. Add raisins around the edges.
3. Create a well for the yeast in the center.
4. Select "Basic Bread" and start. Cool on a wire rack after baking.

# Maple Pecan Loaf

*Ingredients:*

- 280 ml warm water
- 30 ml maple syrup
- 450 g bread flour
- 5 g salt
- 100 g chopped pecans
- 2 1/2 teaspoons bread machine yeast

*Method:*

1. Combine warm water and maple syrup in the bread machine pan.
2. Add flour and salt. Place pecans around the edges.
3. Make a center well for the yeast.
4. Choose the "Basic Bread" setting and start. Allow to cool once baked.

# Oats and Honey Bread

*Ingredients:*

- 280 ml warm water
- 50 g oats
- 30 ml honey
- 420 g bread flour
- 5 g salt
- 2 1/2 teaspoons bread machine yeast

*Method:*

1. Pour water, oats, and honey into the pan.
2. Top with flour and salt.
3. Create a well for the yeast in the center.
4. Set to "Basic Bread" and start. Cool on a rack after baking.

# Almond and Apricot Loaf

*Ingredients:*

- 300 ml warm water
- 450 g bread flour
- 5 g salt
- 5 g sugar
- 100 g dried apricots, chopped
- 70 g sliced almonds
- 2 1/2 teaspoons bread machine yeast

*Method:*

1. Start with warm water in the machine pan.
2. Add flour, sugar, and salt. Place apricots and almonds around the edges.
3. Make a well for the yeast in the center.
4. Use the "Basic Bread" setting and start. Once baked, cool on a rack.

# Chocolate Chip Breakfast Bread

*Ingredients:*

- 300 ml warm water
- 450 g bread flour
- 5 g salt
- 5 g sugar
- 150 g chocolate chips
- 2 1/2 teaspoons bread machine yeast

*Method:*

1. Pour warm water into the bread machine pan.
2. Add flour, sugar, and salt. Place chocolate chips around the edges.
3. Create a center well for the yeast.
4. Set to "Basic Bread" and start. Cool on a wire rack after baking.

# Blueberry Lemon Loaf

*Ingredients:*

- 280 ml warm water
- 30 ml lemon juice
- Zest of 1 lemon
- 450 g bread flour
- 5 g salt
- 5 g sugar
- 100 g fresh blueberries
- 2 1/2 teaspoons bread machine yeast

*Method:*

1. Combine water, lemon juice, and zest in the machine pan.
2. Add flour, sugar, and salt. Sprinkle blueberries around the edges.
3. Make a well in the center for the yeast.
4. Select "Basic Bread" and start. Cool on a wire rack once done.

# Banana Nut Bread

*Ingredients:*

- 2 ripe bananas, mashed (approximately 200 ml)
- 100 ml warm water
- 450 g bread flour
- 5 g salt
- 5 g sugar
- 100 g walnuts, chopped
- 2 1/2 teaspoons bread machine yeast

*Method:*

1. Add mashed bananas and warm water to the bread machine pan.
2. Top with flour, sugar, and salt. Add chopped walnuts around the perimeter.
3. Create a well for the yeast.
4. Use the "Basic Bread" setting and start. Once baked, allow to cool.

# Coffee Caramel Loaf

*Ingredients:*

- 200 ml warm coffee
- 100 ml caramel sauce
- 450 g bread flour
- 5 g salt
- 2 1/2 teaspoons bread machine yeast

*Method:*

1. Pour warm coffee and caramel sauce into the bread machine pan.
2. Add flour and salt.
3. Make a well in the center for the yeast.
4. Set the machine to "Basic Bread" and start. Cool on a wire rack post-baking.

# Vanilla Bean and Cherry Bread

*Ingredients:*

- 300 ml warm water
- 1 vanilla bean, seeds scraped
- 450 g bread flour
- 5 g salt
- 5 g sugar
- 100 g dried cherries
- 2 1/2 teaspoons bread machine yeast

*Method:*

1. Combine warm water and vanilla bean seeds in the pan.
2. Add flour, sugar, and salt. Place cherries around the edges.
3. Create a well for the yeast in the center.
4. Use the "Basic Bread" setting and start. Once baked, cool on a rack.

# Cranberry Walnut Bread

*Ingredients:*

- 300 ml warm water
- 450 g bread flour
- 5 g salt
- 5 g sugar
- 100 g dried cranberries
- 100 g walnuts, chopped
- 2 1/2 teaspoons bread machine yeast

*Method:*

1. Start with warm water in the machine pan.
2. Top with flour, sugar, and salt. Add cranberries and walnuts around the edges.
3. Create a well in the center for the yeast.
4. Set to "Basic Bread" and start. Cool on a wire rack post-baking.

# Coconut Pineapple Loaf

*Ingredients:*

- 240 ml warm water
- 60 ml pineapple juice
- 450 g bread flour
- 5 g salt
- 5 g sugar
- 50 g shredded coconut
- 2 1/2 teaspoons bread machine yeast

*Method:*

1. Combine warm water and pineapple juice in the bread machine pan.
2. Add flour, sugar, and salt. Sprinkle coconut around the edges.
3. Create a well for the yeast in the center.
4. Use the "Basic Bread" setting and start. Allow to cool after baking.

# Apple Cinnamon Loaf

*Ingredients:*

- 240 ml warm water
- 60 ml apple juice
- 450 g bread flour
- 5 g salt
- 10 g sugar
- 2 g cinnamon
- 100 g dried apples, chopped
- 2 1/2 teaspoons bread machine yeast

*Method:*

1. Pour warm water and apple juice into the bread machine pan.
2. Add flour, sugar, salt, and cinnamon. Add chopped apples around the edges.
3. Make a well for the yeast in the center.
4. Set to "Basic Bread" and start. Cool on a wire rack post-baking.

# Peanut Butter Breakfast Bread

*Ingredients:*

- 200 ml warm water
- 100 ml peanut butter (smooth or chunky)
- 450 g bread flour
- 5 g salt
- 2 1/2 teaspoons bread machine yeast

*Method:*

1. Mix warm water and peanut butter in the bread machine pan until smooth.
2. Add flour and salt.
3. Create a well in the center for the yeast.
4. Choose the "Basic Bread" setting and start. Allow to cool once baked.

Enjoy these wonderful breakfast breads! Adjustments can be made depending on your bread machine's requirements and personal taste preferences.

# CHEESE BREAD RECIPES

## Classic Cheddar Loaf

*Ingredients:*

- 300 ml warm water
- 450 g bread flour
- 5 g salt
- 150 g sharp cheddar cheese, grated
- 2 1/2 teaspoons bread machine yeast

*Method:*

1. Pour warm water into the bread machine pan.
2. Add flour, salt, and then sprinkle the cheese on top.
3. Make a well in the center for the yeast.
4. Choose the "Basic Bread" setting and start. Once baked, allow to cool.

# Parmesan Herb Bread

*Ingredients:*

- 300 ml warm water
- 450 g bread flour
- 5 g salt
- 5 g sugar
- 100 g parmesan cheese, grated
- 5 g dried basil
- 5 g dried oregano
- 2 1/2 teaspoons bread machine yeast

*Method:*

1. Start with warm water in the machine pan.
2. Add flour, sugar, salt, herbs, and parmesan.
3. Create a well for the yeast.
4. Set to "Basic Bread" and start. Allow to cool once done.

## Blue Cheese and Walnut Bread

*Ingredients:*

- 280 ml warm water
- 450 g bread flour
- 5 g salt
- 5 g sugar
- 100 g blue cheese, crumbled
- 70 g walnuts, chopped
- 2 1/2 teaspoons bread machine yeast

*Method:*

1. Pour warm water into the bread machine pan.
2. Add flour, sugar, salt, blue cheese, and walnuts.
3. Create a well in the center for the yeast.
4. Use the "Basic Bread" setting and start. Cool on a rack post-baking.

# Mozzarella and Tomato Loaf

*Ingredients:*

- 280 ml warm water
- 450 g bread flour
- 5 g salt
- 5 g sugar
- 100 g mozzarella cheese, diced
- 70 g sun-dried tomatoes, chopped
- 2 1/2 teaspoons bread machine yeast

*Method:*

1. Begin with warm water in the bread machine pan.
2. Add flour, sugar, salt, mozzarella, and sun-dried tomatoes.
3. Make a well for the yeast in the center.
4. Choose the "Basic Bread" setting and start. Cool on a rack after baking.

# Pepper Jack and Jalapeno Bread

*Ingredients:*

- 300 ml warm water
- 450 g bread flour
- 5 g salt
- 100 g pepper jack cheese, grated
- 30 g jalapenos, chopped (adjust to heat preference)
- 2 1/2 teaspoons bread machine yeast

*Method:*

1. Pour warm water into the pan.
2. Add flour, salt, cheese, and jalapenos.
3. Create a well in the center for the yeast.
4. Set to "Basic Bread" and start. Cool on a wire rack post-baking.

# Garlic and Gouda Loaf

*Ingredients:*

- 300 ml warm water
- 450 g bread flour
- 5 g salt
- 10 g garlic powder
- 100 g gouda cheese, grated
- 2 1/2 teaspoons bread machine yeast

*Method:*

1. Start with warm water in the bread machine pan.
2. Add flour, salt, garlic powder, and gouda.
3. Create a well for the yeast.
4. Choose the "Basic Bread" setting and start. Allow to cool after baking.

# Brie and Cranberry Bread

*Ingredients:*

- 280 ml warm water
- 450 g bread flour
- 5 g salt
- 100 g brie cheese, diced
- 70 g dried cranberries
- 2 1/2 teaspoons bread machine yeast

*Method:*

1. Pour warm water into the pan.
2. Add flour, salt, brie, and cranberries.
3. Make a well in the center for the yeast.
4. Set to "Basic Bread" and start. Cool on a wire rack once baked.

# Cream Cheese and Chive Bread

*Ingredients:*

- 280 ml warm water
- 450 g bread flour
- 5 g salt
- 100 g cream cheese, diced
- 30 g fresh chives, chopped
- 2 1/2 teaspoons bread machine yeast

*Method:*

1. Begin with warm water in the pan.
2. Add flour, salt, cream cheese, and chives.
3. Create a well for the yeast in the center.
4. Use the "Basic Bread" setting and start. Allow to cool once baked.

## Goat Cheese and Rosemary Bread

*Ingredients:*

- 300 ml warm water
- 450 g bread flour
- 5 g salt
- 100 g goat cheese, crumbled
- 5 g dried rosemary
- 2 1/2 teaspoons bread machine yeast

*Method:*

1. Pour warm water into the bread machine pan.
2. Add flour, salt, goat cheese, and rosemary.
3. Create a well in the center for the yeast.
4. Choose the "Basic Bread" setting and start. Cool on a rack post-baking.

# Swiss Cheese and Onion Bread

*Ingredients:*

- 280 ml warm water
- 450 g bread flour
- 5 g salt
- 5 g sugar
- 100 g Swiss cheese, grated
- 50 g dried minced onion
- 2 1/2 teaspoons bread machine yeast

*Method:*

1. Start with warm water in the pan.
2. Add flour, sugar, salt, Swiss cheese, and onion.
3. Make a well for the yeast.
4. Set to "Basic Bread" and start. Allow to cool once baked.

## Feta and Olive Bread

*Ingredients:*

- 300 ml warm water
- 450 g bread flour
- 5 g salt
- 100 g feta cheese, crumbled
- 70 g olives, pitted and chopped (green or black, as preferred)
- 2 1/2 teaspoons bread machine yeast

*Method:*

1. Pour warm water into the bread machine pan.
2. Add flour, salt, feta, and olives.
3. Create a well for the yeast in the center.
4. Use the "Basic Bread" setting and start. Cool on a wire rack after baking.

## Provolone and Pesto Bread

*Ingredients:*

- 260 ml warm water
- 40 ml pesto sauce
- 450 g bread flour
- 5 g salt
- 100 g provolone cheese, diced
- 2 1/2 teaspoons bread machine yeast

*Method:*

1. Combine warm water and pesto in the bread machine pan.
2. Add flour, salt, and provolone.
3. Create a well in the center
4. Use the "Basic Bread" setting and start. Cool on a wire rack after baking.

# SOURDOUGH BREAD RECIPES

## Classic Sourdough

*Ingredients:*

- 240ml water
- 120g sourdough starter
- 360g bread flour
- 8g salt
- 8g sugar

*Instructions:*

1. Place all ingredients in the bread machine pan in the order listed.
2. Select the basic bread setting, choose the crust color you desire, and start the machine.
3. Once done, remove the bread and let cool on a wire rack.

## Whole Wheat Sourdough

*Ingredients:*

- 240ml water
- 120g sourdough starter
- 270g whole wheat flour
- 90g bread flour
- 8g salt
- 10g sugar

*Instructions:*

1. Follow the same instructions as the Classic Sourdough.

## Rye Sourdough Bread

*Ingredients:*

- 230ml water
- 130g sourdough starter
- 270g rye flour
- 90g bread flour
- 8g salt
- 10g caraway seeds (optional)

*Instructions:*

1. Follow the Classic Sourdough instructions.

## Olive Rosemary Sourdough

*Ingredients:*

- 240ml water
- 120g sourdough starter
- 350g bread flour
- 8g salt
- 10g sugar
- 50g chopped olives
- 2 tsp chopped rosemary

*Instructions:*

1. Add olives and rosemary after the initial mixing or when the machine beeps for additions.
2. Follow the Classic Sourdough instructions.

## Garlic Herb Sourdough

*Ingredients:*

- 240ml water
- 120g sourdough starter
- 360g bread flour
- 8g salt
- 10g sugar
- 3 minced garlic cloves
- 2 tsp mixed dried herbs (thyme, basil, oregano)

*Instructions:*

1. Follow the Classic Sourdough instructions.

## Honey Oat Sourdough

*Ingredients:*

- 240ml water
- 130g sourdough starter
- 320g bread flour
- 50g oats
- 8g salt
- 25g honey

*Instructions:*

1. Follow the Classic Sourdough instructions.

## Seeded Multigrain Sourdough

*Ingredients:*

- 240ml water
- 120g sourdough starter
- 270g bread flour
- 90g multigrain mix
- 8g salt

- 15g sugar
- 40g mixed seeds (sunflower, sesame, flax)

*Instructions:*

1. Follow the Classic Sourdough instructions.

## Chocolate Chip & Walnut Sourdough

*Ingredients:*

- 240ml water
- 120g sourdough starter
- 350g bread flour
- 8g salt
- 25g sugar
- 80g chocolate chips
- 50g chopped walnuts

*Instructions:*

1. Add chocolate chips and walnuts after the initial mixing.
2. Follow the Classic Sourdough instructions.

# Spiced Fruit Sourdough

*Ingredients:*

- 240ml water
- 120g sourdough starter
- 360g bread flour
- 8g salt
- 25g sugar
- 1 tsp cinnamon
- 1/2 tsp nutmeg
- 100g mixed dried fruit

*Instructions:*

1. Follow the Classic Sourdough instructions.

# Cheese & Chive Sourdough

*Ingredients:*

- 240ml water
- 120g sourdough starter
- 350g bread flour
- 8g salt
- 10g sugar
- 90g grated cheese (cheddar or your choice)

- 2 tbsp chopped chives

*Instructions:*

1. Follow the Classic Sourdough instructions.

## Cinnamon Raisin Sourdough

*Ingredients:*

- 240ml water
- 120g sourdough starter
- 340g bread flour
- 8g salt
- 25g sugar
- 1.5 tsp cinnamon
- 100g raisins

*Instructions:*

1. Follow the Classic Sourdough instructions.

# Jalapeño Cheddar Sourdough

*Ingredients:*

- 240ml water
- 120g sourdough starter
- 350g bread flour
- 8g salt
- 10g sugar
- 2 chopped jalapeños (de-seeded)
- 90g grated cheddar cheese

*Instructions:*

1. Follow the Classic Sourdough instructions.

# Sun-dried Tomato & Basil Sourdough

*Ingredients:*

- 240ml water
- 120g sourdough starter
- 340g bread flour
- 8g salt
- 10g sugar
- 60g chopped sun-dried tomatoes

- 2 tsp dried basil

*Instructions:*

1. Follow the Classic Sourdough instructions.

For optimal results, always ensure your sourdough starter is active and bubbly before using it in a recipe. Also, check your bread machine's manual to see if it recommends a particular order for adding ingredients. Adjust as needed. Enjoy your sourdough adventures!

# Gluten-free bread recipes

## Basic White Gluten-Free Bread

*Ingredients:*

- 400 gr gluten-free bread flour mix
- 250 ml warm water
- 1 tablespoon sugar
- 2 teaspoons active dry yeast
- 1 teaspoon salt
- 2 tablespoons olive oil
- 1 teaspoon apple cider vinegar

*Instructions:*

1. Pour the warm water into the bread machine pan. Sprinkle the sugar and then the yeast on top of the water. Let it sit for about 10 minutes or until frothy.
2. Add the flour, salt, olive oil, and apple cider vinegar to the pan.
3. Set the bread machine to the gluten-free setting, select a medium crust, and press start.

# Brown Rice Bread

*Ingredients:*

- 340 gr brown rice flour
- 60 gr potato starch
- 1 tablespoon xanthan gum
- 250 ml warm water
- 2 teaspoons active dry yeast
- 2 tablespoons honey
- 1 teaspoon salt
- 2 tablespoons olive oil
- 2 eggs

*Instructions:*

1. Combine the warm water, honey, and yeast in the bread machine pan. Allow it to sit for 10 minutes.
2. Add the brown rice flour, potato starch, xanthan gum, salt, olive oil, and eggs.
3. Set the bread machine to the gluten-free setting, choose a medium crust, and start.

# Quinoa Bread

*Ingredients:*

- 230 gr quinoa flour
- 170 gr tapioca flour
- 250 ml warm water
- 2 teaspoons yeast
- 2 tablespoons honey
- 2 tablespoons olive oil
- 1 teaspoon salt
- 1 teaspoon apple cider vinegar

*Instructions:*

1. Mix the warm water, honey, and yeast in the bread machine pan and let sit for 10 minutes.
2. Add the quinoa flour, tapioca flour, olive oil, salt, and apple cider vinegar.
3. Set to the gluten-free setting, select a medium crust, and start.

# Teff Bread

*Ingredients:*

- 290 gr teff flour
- 110 gr tapioca flour
- 250 ml warm water
- 2 teaspoons active dry yeast
- 1 tablespoon honey
- 2 tablespoons olive oil
- 1 teaspoon salt
- 2 eggs

*Instructions:*

1. In the bread machine pan, mix warm water, honey, and yeast. Let sit for 10 minutes.
2. Add the flours, olive oil, salt, and eggs.
3. Use the gluten-free setting, select a medium crust, and press start.

# Buckwheat Bread

*Ingredients:*

- 290 gr buckwheat flour
- 110 gr potato starch
- 1 tablespoon xanthan gum
- 250 ml warm water
- 2 teaspoons yeast
- 2 tablespoons honey
- 1 teaspoon salt
- 2 tablespoons olive oil
- 1 teaspoon apple cider vinegar

*Instructions:*

1. Mix warm water, honey, and yeast in the bread machine pan. Wait 10 minutes.
2. Add remaining ingredients.
3. Choose the gluten-free setting, a medium crust, and start.

# Almond Bread

*Ingredients:*

- 200 gr almond flour
- 200 gr tapioca flour
- 1 tablespoon xanthan gum
- 250 ml warm water
- 2 teaspoons yeast
- 2 tablespoons honey
- 2 tablespoons olive oil
- 1 teaspoon salt

*Instructions:*

1. In the bread machine pan, combine warm water, honey, and yeast. Let sit for 10 minutes.
2. Add the flours, xanthan gum, olive oil, and salt.
3. Use the gluten-free setting, choose a medium crust, and press start.

# Millet Bread

*Ingredients:*

- 290 gr millet flour
- 110 gr tapioca flour
- 250 ml warm water
- 2 teaspoons yeast
- 1 tablespoon honey
- 1 teaspoon salt
- 2 tablespoons olive oil
- 1 teaspoon apple cider vinegar

*Instructions:*

1. Mix warm water, honey, and yeast in the bread machine pan and wait 10 minutes.
2. Add the flours, salt, olive oil, and apple cider vinegar.
3. Use the gluten-free setting, choose a medium crust, and press start.

# Sorghum Bread

*Ingredients:*

- 290 gr sorghum flour
- 110 gr potato starch
- 1 tablespoon xanthan gum
- 250 ml warm water
- 2 teaspoons yeast
- 2 tablespoons honey
- 1 teaspoon salt
- 2 tablespoons olive oil
- 2 eggs

*Instructions:*

1. Combine warm water, honey, and yeast in the bread machine pan. Wait for 10 minutes.
2. Add the remaining ingredients.

3. Set the machine to the gluten-free setting, select a medium crust, and start.

# Coconut Bread

*Ingredients:*

- 200 gr coconut flour
- 200 gr tapioca flour
- 1 tablespoon xanthan gum
- 250 ml warm water
- 2 teaspoons yeast
- 2 tablespoons honey
- 2 tablespoons coconut oil
- 1 teaspoon salt

*Instructions:*

1. Mix warm water, honey, and yeast in the bread machine pan. Let sit for 10 minutes.
2. Add the remaining ingredients.
3. Use the gluten-free setting, choose a medium crust, and press start.

# Oat Bread (ensure GF oats)

*Ingredients:*

- 400 gr gluten-free oat flour
- 250 ml warm water
- 2 teaspoons yeast
- 1 tablespoon honey
- 1 teaspoon salt
- 2 tablespoons olive oil

*Instructions:*

1. Combine warm water, honey, and yeast in the bread machine pan. Wait 10 minutes.
2. Add oat flour, salt, and olive oil.
3. Set to the gluten-free setting, select a medium crust, and start.

# Chestnut Bread

*Ingredients:*

- 290 gr chestnut flour
- 110 gr tapioca flour
- 1 tablespoon xanthan gum
- 250 ml warm water
- 2 teaspoons yeast
- 2 tablespoons honey
- 1 teaspoon salt
- 2 tablespoons olive oil

*Instructions:*

1. Mix warm water, honey, and yeast in the bread machine pan. Let it sit for 10 minutes.
2. Add the flours, xanthan gum, salt, and olive oil.
3. Use the gluten-free setting, choose a medium crust, and start.

# Corn Bread

*Ingredients:*

- 400 gr cornmeal
- 250 ml warm water
- 2 teaspoons yeast
- 2 tablespoons honey
- 1 teaspoon salt
- 2 tablespoons olive oil

*Instructions:*

1. Combine warm water, honey, and yeast in the bread machine pan. Wait 10 minutes.
2. Add cornmeal, salt, and olive oil.
3. Use the gluten-free setting, choose a medium crust, and press start.

# Chia Seed Bread

*Ingredients:*

- 290 gr gluten-free flour mix
- 60 gr chia seeds
- 250 ml warm water
- 2 teaspoons yeast
- 2 tablespoons honey
- 1 teaspoon salt
- 2 tablespoons olive oil
- 2 eggs

*Instructions:*

1. Mix warm water, honey, and yeast in the bread machine pan. Wait for 10 minutes.
2. Add the flour, chia seeds, salt, olive oil, and eggs.
3. Set the bread machine to the gluten-free setting, select a medium crust, and start.

Note: Always check the manufacturer's instructions for your bread machine, as some machines may have specific requirements or steps for gluten-free bread.

# PIZZA AND FOCACCIA

## Classic Pizza Dough

*Ingredients:*

- 500 gr all-purpose flour
- 250 ml warm water
- 2 teaspoons active dry yeast
- 2 tablespoons olive oil
- 1 teaspoon sugar
- 1 teaspoon salt

*Instructions:*

1. Add water, sugar, and yeast to the bread machine pan. Let it sit for 10 minutes.
2. Add flour, olive oil, and salt.
3. Set the machine to the dough setting and start.
4. Once done, roll out the dough, add toppings, and bake at 220°C for 12-15 minutes.

*Tip:* For a crispier crust, pre-bake the dough for 5 minutes before adding toppings.

# Whole Wheat Pizza Dough

*Ingredients:*

- 375 gr whole wheat flour
- 125 gr all-purpose flour
- 270 ml warm water
- 2 teaspoons yeast
- 1 teaspoon sugar
- 2 tablespoons olive oil
- 1 teaspoon salt

*Instructions:*

1. Add water, sugar, and yeast to the bread machine pan. Let it sit for 10 minutes.
2. Add flour, olive oil, and salt.
3. Set the machine to the dough setting and start.
4. Once done, roll out the dough, add toppings, and bake at 220°C for 12-15 minutes.

# Herb-Infused Focaccia

*Ingredients:*

- 500 gr all-purpose flour
- 310 ml warm water
- 2 teaspoons yeast
- 2 tablespoons olive oil
- 1 teaspoon sugar
- 1 teaspoon salt
- 1 tablespoon mixed herbs (rosemary, thyme, oregano)

*Instructions:*

1. Follow the same steps as the Classic Pizza Dough.
2. After the dough cycle completes, press into a rectangular pan.
3. Drizzle with more olive oil and sprinkle with herbs.
4. Bake at 220°C for 20-25 minutes.

*Secret:* Brush with garlic-infused olive oil for added flavor.

# Garlic Focaccia

*Ingredients:*

- 500 gr all-purpose flour
- 310 ml warm water
- 2 teaspoons yeast
- 2 tablespoons olive oil
- 2 teaspoons crushed garlic
- 1 teaspoon sugar
- 1 teaspoon salt

*Instructions:* Follow the same steps as Herb-Infused Focaccia.

# Stuffed Crust Pizza

*Ingredients:*

- 500 gr all-purpose flour
- 250 ml warm water
- 2 teaspoons yeast
- 2 tablespoons olive oil
- 1 teaspoon sugar
- 1 teaspoon salt
- 150 gr mozzarella cheese, cut into small sticks

*Instructions:*

1. Follow steps 1-3 of the Classic Pizza Dough.
2. Roll out the dough larger than required. Place cheese sticks around the edge, fold dough over the cheese and press to seal.
3. Add toppings and bake at 220°C for 15-18 minutes.

*Tip:* Use fresh mozzarella for a melt-in-the-mouth experience.

## Olive Focaccia

*Ingredients:*

- 500 gr all-purpose flour
- 310 ml warm water
- 2 teaspoons yeast
- 2 tablespoons olive oil
- 1 teaspoon sugar
- 1 teaspoon salt
- 100 gr chopped olives

*Instructions:* Follow the same steps as Herb-Infused Focaccia, adding olives before baking.

# Thin Crust Pizza Dough

*Ingredients:*

- 400 gr all-purpose flour
- 230 ml warm water
- 2 teaspoons yeast
- 1 tablespoon olive oil
- 1 teaspoon sugar
- 1 teaspoon salt

*Instructions:* Follow the same steps as the Classic Pizza Dough.

*Secret:* Rolling the dough between two sheets of parchment paper helps achieve an even, thin crust.

# Cheese Focaccia

*Ingredients:*

- 500 gr all-purpose flour
- 310 ml warm water
- 2 teaspoons yeast
- 2 tablespoons olive oil
- 1 teaspoon sugar
- 1 teaspoon salt
- 150 gr grated cheese (like Parmesan or Asiago)

*Instructions:* Follow the same steps as Herb-Infused Focaccia, sprinkling cheese before baking.

# Gluten-Free Pizza Dough

*Ingredients:*

- 400 gr gluten-free flour blend
- 250 ml warm water
- 2 teaspoons yeast
- 2 tablespoons olive oil
- 1 teaspoon sugar
- 1 teaspoon salt

*Instructions:* Follow the same steps as the Classic Pizza Dough.


# Multi-Grain Pizza Dough

*Ingredients:*

- 250 gr all-purpose flour
- 125 gr whole wheat flour
- 125 gr rye flour
- 270 ml warm water
- 2 teaspoons yeast
- 2 tablespoons olive oil
- 1 teaspoon sugar
- 1 teaspoon salt

*Instructions:* Follow the same steps as the Classic Pizza Dough.

*Tip:* You can vary the flour ratios to suit your taste.

# Onion Focaccia

*Ingredients:*

- 500 gr all-purpose flour
- 310 ml warm water
- 2 teaspoons yeast
- 2 tablespoons olive oil
- 1 teaspoon sugar
- 1 teaspoon salt
- 1 large onion, thinly sliced

*Instructions:* Follow the same steps as Herb-Infused Focaccia, topping with onion slices before baking.


# Sourdough Pizza Dough

*Ingredients:*

- 400 gr all-purpose flour
- 200 ml sourdough starter
- 150 ml warm water
- 2 tablespoons olive oil
- 1 teaspoon salt

*Instructions:*

1. Combine starter, water, and oil in the bread machine pan.
2. Add flour and salt.
3. Use the dough setting on the machine.
4. Roll, add toppings, and bake at 220°C for 12-15 minutes.

## Sun-Dried Tomato Focaccia

*Ingredients:*

- 500 gr all-purpose flour
- 310 ml warm water
- 2 teaspoons yeast
- 2 tablespoons olive oil
- 1 teaspoon sugar
- 1 teaspoon salt
- 100 gr chopped sun-dried tomatoes

*Instructions:* Follow the same steps as Herb-Infused Focaccia, adding sun-dried tomatoes before baking.

*Tip:* Use sun-dried tomatoes that have been soaked in oil for added moisture and flavor.

**Secret for All Recipes:** Always allow your baked pizza or focaccia to rest for a few minutes after taking out of the oven. This will help in settling the flavors and makes slicing easier.

# BONUS Breads from Around the World – European bread recipes

Every culture has its own relationship with bread. It's a universal food but takes on different forms, flavors, and techniques depending on where you are in the world.

Take the French Baguette, for instance. A symbol of French culture, the Baguette is slender, with a crisp crust encasing a soft, airy crumb. It's the result of a delicate interplay between the simplest of ingredients: flour, water, yeast, and salt. The key to a great Baguette lies in its fermentation, often requiring multiple stages to develop its characteristic flavor and texture.

Then we travel to Italy, where Ciabatta steals the show. This rustic bread, with its uneven holes and moist crumb, is a testament to Italian baking prowess. Ciabatta, which translates to "slipper" in Italian due to its shape, is ideal for sandwiches or simply to mop up delicious pasta sauces.

But bread isn't just limited to Europe. In the Middle East, Pita bread plays a central role. This round, pocketed bread is a staple in many meals, perfect for scooping up hummus or as a wrap for kebabs. Pita's unique shape results from the rapid puffing up of the dough during baking, creating a hollow center.

Each of these breads, though distinct in flavor, texture, and appearance, underscores the universality of bread and its significance across cultures. Through this chapter, you'll not only learn the techniques to create these global delights but also gain an appreciation for the rich tapestry of stories and traditions they carry with them.

# French Baguette

*Ingredients:*

- 500 gr all-purpose flour
- 300 ml warm water
- 2 teaspoons active dry yeast
- 2 teaspoons salt
- 1 teaspoon sugar

*Instructions:*

1. Add water, sugar, and yeast to the bread machine pan and let sit for 10 minutes.
2. Add flour and salt.
3. Set the machine to the dough setting.
4. Once done, shape into a long loaf and let rise for 30 minutes.
5. Bake at 220°C for 25 minutes or until golden brown.

*Tip:* For a crispier crust, mist with water before baking.


# Italian Ciabatta

*Ingredients:*

- 500 gr bread flour
- 340 ml warm water
- 2 teaspoons active dry yeast
- 2 teaspoons salt

*Instructions:* Follow the same steps as the French Baguette.

*Tip:* This dough is stickier than most. Wet your hands slightly when shaping.

## German Rye Bread

*Ingredients:*

- 300 gr rye flour
- 200 gr all-purpose flour
- 300 ml warm water
- 2 teaspoons active dry yeast
- 2 teaspoons salt
- 2 tablespoons molasses

*Instructions:*

1. Add water, molasses, and yeast to the bread machine pan. Let sit for 10 minutes.
2. Add flours and salt.
3. Set the machine to the whole grain setting.
4. Once done, let the bread cool completely.

*Tip:* Rye breads have a denser texture. Slice them thinly for best results.

## British Cottage Loaf

*Ingredients:*

- 500 gr bread flour
- 300 ml warm water
- 2 teaspoons active dry yeast
- 2 teaspoons salt
- 1 teaspoon sugar
- 2 tablespoons unsalted butter

*Instructions:*

1. Add water, sugar, and yeast to the bread machine pan. Wait for 10 minutes.
2. Add flour, butter, and salt.
3. Set machine to basic bread setting.

*Tip:* This bread has a firm crust and soft inside, making it great for sandwiches.

## Irish Soda Bread

*Ingredients:*

- 500 gr all-purpose flour
- 400 ml buttermilk
- 1 teaspoon baking soda
- 1 teaspoon salt

*Instructions:*

1. Add all ingredients to the bread machine pan.
2. Set machine to the quick bread or cake setting.
3. Once done, let the bread cool completely.

*Tip:* Serve with butter or jam.

## Portuguese Sweet Bread

*Ingredients:*

- 500 gr all-purpose flour
- 120 ml milk
- 2 teaspoons active dry yeast
- 75 gr sugar
- 50 gr unsalted butter, softened
- 2 eggs
- 1 teaspoon salt

*Instructions:*

1. Add milk, sugar, and yeast to the bread machine pan. Let sit for 10 minutes.
2. Add remaining ingredients.
3. Set machine to the sweet bread setting.

*Tip:* This bread is best enjoyed fresh with butter.

# Dutch Crunch Bread

*Ingredients:*

- 500 gr bread flour
- 300 ml warm water
- 2 teaspoons active dry yeast
- 2 teaspoons salt
- 1 teaspoon sugar

*Topping:*

- 60 gr rice flour
- 120 ml warm water
- 1 tablespoon sugar
- 1 tablespoon vegetable oil
- 1 teaspoon active dry yeast

*Instructions:*

1. Add water, sugar, and yeast to the bread machine pan. Wait for 10 minutes.
2. Add flour and salt.
3. Set machine to dough setting.
4. Once done, shape into a loaf and let rise.
5. Mix all topping ingredients and spread over the loaf.
6. Bake at 190°C for 25-30 minutes.

*Tip:* The unique topping cracks during baking, creating the signature "crunch".

## Austrian Potato Bread

*Ingredients:*

- 400 gr bread flour
- 100 gr mashed potatoes
- 240 ml warm water
- 2 teaspoons active dry yeast
- 2 teaspoons salt

*Instructions:* Follow the same steps as the French Baguette.

*Tip:* Potato makes this bread moist. Store in an airtight container.

## Spanish Barra Gallega

*Ingredients:*

- 500 gr bread flour
- 320 ml warm water
- 2 teaspoons active dry yeast
- 2 teaspoons salt

*Instructions:* Follow the same steps as the French Baguette.

*Tip:* This bread has a distinct chewy crust, great with Spanish tapas.

## Swedish Limpa Bread

*Ingredients:*

- 250 gr rye flour
- 250 gr all-purpose flour
- 240 ml warm water
- 2 teaspoons active dry yeast
- 50 gr brown sugar
- 2 tablespoons unsalted butter
- 1 tablespoon orange zest
- 2 teaspoons caraway seeds
- 1 teaspoon salt

*Instructions:*

1. Add water, brown sugar, and yeast to the bread machine pan. Let sit for 10 minutes.
2. Add remaining ingredients.
3. Set machine to whole grain or basic setting.

*Tip:* The orange zest and caraway seeds give a distinctive taste. Adjust according to preference.

## Belgian Pain de Campagne (Country Bread)

*Ingredients:*

- 375 gr bread flour
- 125 gr whole wheat flour
- 300 ml warm water
- 2 teaspoons active dry yeast
- 2 teaspoons salt

*Instructions:* Follow the same steps as the French Baguette.

*Tip:* This bread has a rustic crust. It pairs well with hearty stews.


## Greek Olive Bread (Eliopsomo)

*Ingredients:*

- 500 gr bread flour
- 300 ml warm water
- 2 teaspoons active dry yeast
- 2 teaspoons salt
- 150 gr Kalamata olives, pitted and chopped
- 1 tablespoon olive oil

*Instructions:*

1. Add water, and yeast to the bread machine pan. Wait for 10 minutes.
2. Add flour, salt, olives, and olive oil.
3. Set machine to basic bread setting.

*Tip:* Serve with olive oil and balsamic vinegar for dipping.

**General Secret for All Recipes:** Always use the freshest ingredients for the best results. If your bread machine has an option for a light crust, it's often the best choice for European breads to ensure they don't turn out too hard or thick.

# BONUS AMERICAN HOLIDAY BREAD RECIPES

## Thanksgiving Pumpkin Bread

*Ingredients:*

- 450 gr bread flour
- 200 ml pumpkin puree
- 100 ml warm water
- 2 teaspoons active dry yeast
- 50 gr brown sugar
- 1 teaspoon salt
- 1 teaspoon cinnamon
- 1/2 teaspoon nutmeg
- 1/4 teaspoon cloves

*Instructions:*

1. Add water, pumpkin puree, sugar, and yeast to the bread machine pan. Wait for 10 minutes.
2. Add flour, salt, and spices.
3. Set machine to basic bread setting.

*Tip:* For added texture, fold in 100 gr of roasted pumpkin seeds before baking.

# Christmas Stollen

*Ingredients:*

- 450 gr bread flour
- 120 ml warm milk
- 2 teaspoons active dry yeast
- 100 gr unsalted butter, softened
- 75 gr sugar
- 1 teaspoon salt
- 150 gr mixed dried fruits (raisins, currants, candied citrus)
- 50 gr chopped almonds
- 1 teaspoon vanilla extract

*Instructions:*

1. Add milk, butter, sugar, and yeast to the bread machine pan. Let sit for 10 minutes.
2. Add remaining ingredients.
3. Set machine to fruit/nut bread setting or basic setting.

*Tip:* Dust with powdered sugar after baking for a festive look.

# Easter Hot Cross Buns

*Ingredients:*

- 450 gr bread flour
- 240 ml warm milk
- 2 teaspoons active dry yeast
- 75 gr sugar
- 50 gr unsalted butter, melted
- 1 egg
- 1 teaspoon salt
- 1 teaspoon cinnamon
- 150 gr currants or raisins

*Instructions:*

1. Add milk, butter, sugar, and yeast to the bread machine pan. Wait for 10 minutes.
2. Add egg, flour, salt, and cinnamon.
3. Set machine to dough setting.
4. Once done, shape into buns, let rise, then bake at 190°C for 20 minutes.
5. Use icing to make a cross on each bun after baking.

*Tip:* For the icing, mix powdered sugar with a bit of milk.

## Fourth of July American Flag Bread

*Ingredients:*

- 500 gr bread flour
- 270 ml warm water
- 2 teaspoons active dry yeast
- 2 teaspoons salt
- Red and blue food coloring

*Instructions:*

1. Add water, and yeast to the bread machine pan. Wait for 10 minutes.
2. Add flour and salt.
3. Set machine to dough setting.
4. Once done, divide the dough into three parts. Color one part red and another part blue.
5. Shape and layer the colored doughs in a loaf pan.
6. Let rise, then bake at 190°C for 30 minutes.

*Tip:* This bread is more about appearance than flavor. Serve sliced at picnics!

# New Year's Champagne Bread

*Ingredients:*

- 450 gr bread flour
- 240 ml champagne, warmed slightly
- 2 teaspoons active dry yeast
- 50 gr sugar
- 1 teaspoon salt

*Instructions:*

1. Add champagne, sugar, and yeast to the bread machine pan. Let sit for 10 minutes.
2. Add flour and salt.
3. Set machine to basic bread setting.

*Tip:* This bread has a unique, slightly tangy flavor due to the champagne.

# Valentine's Day Chocolate Bread

*Ingredients:*

- 450 gr bread flour
- 240 ml warm milk
- 2 teaspoons active dry yeast
- 75 gr sugar
- 50 gr cocoa powder
- 100 gr chocolate chips

*Instructions:*

1. Add milk, sugar, cocoa, and yeast to the bread machine pan. Let sit for 10 minutes.
2. Add flour.
3. Set machine to basic bread setting, adding chocolate chips when the machine beeps for mix-ins.

*Tip:* Serve slices with strawberries for a romantic touch.

# Memorial Day Walnut Bread

*Ingredients:*

- 450 gr bread flour
- 240 ml warm water
- 2 teaspoons active dry yeast
- 50 gr sugar
- 1 teaspoon salt
- 150 gr chopped walnuts

*Instructions:*

1. Add water, sugar, and yeast to the bread machine pan. Wait for 10 minutes.
2. Add flour, salt, and walnuts.
3. Set machine to basic bread setting.

*Tip:* Pair with blue cheese for a flavorful snack.

## Halloween Spiced Bread

*Ingredients:*

- 450 gr bread flour
- 240 ml warm water
- 2 teaspoons active dry yeast
- 75 gr brown sugar
- 1 teaspoon salt
- 2 teaspoons pumpkin pie spice

*Instructions:*

1. Add water, sugar, and yeast to the bread machine pan. Wait for 10 minutes.
2. Add flour, salt, and spice.
3. Set machine to basic bread setting.

*Tip:* Use Halloween-themed cookie cutters on the bread for festive sandwiches.

# Labor Day Cornbread

*Ingredients:*

- 300 gr bread flour
- 200 gr cornmeal
- 240 ml warm milk
- 2 teaspoons active dry yeast
- 50 gr sugar
- 1 teaspoon salt

*Instructions:*

1. Add milk, sugar, and yeast to the bread machine pan. Wait for 10 minutes.
2. Add flour, cornmeal, and salt.
3. Set machine to basic bread setting.

*Tip:* Serve with chili or barbecued meats.

# Martin Luther King Jr. Day Pecan Bread

*Ingredients:*

- 450 gr bread flour
- 240 ml warm milk
- 2 teaspoons active dry yeast
- 75 gr brown sugar
- 1 teaspoon salt
- 150 gr chopped pecans

*Instructions:*

1. Add milk, sugar, and yeast to the bread machine pan. Wait for 10 minutes.
2. Add flour, salt, and pecans.
3. Set machine to basic bread setting.

*Tip:* This bread is rich and slightly sweet. It pairs well with coffee.

# Veteran's Day Multi-grain Bread

*Ingredients:*

- 300 gr bread flour
- 100 gr whole wheat flour
- 50 gr oats
- 50 gr flaxseed
- 270 ml warm water
- 2 teaspoons active dry yeast
- 1 teaspoon salt

*Instructions:*

1. Add water, and yeast to the bread machine pan. Wait for 10 minutes.
2. Add flours, oats, flaxseed, and salt.
3. Set machine to whole grain setting.

*Tip:* This hearty bread is packed with nutrients. Toast slices for added crunch.

# President's Day Cherry Almond Bread

*Ingredients:*

- 450 gr bread flour
- 240 ml warm milk
- 2 teaspoons active dry yeast
- 75 gr sugar
- 1 teaspoon salt
- 100 gr dried cherries
- 100 gr chopped almonds

*Instructions:*

1. Add milk, sugar, and yeast to the bread machine pan. Wait for 10 minutes.
2. Add flour, salt, cherries, and almonds.
3. Set machine to fruit/nut bread setting or basic setting.

*Tip:* This bread has a delightful fruity and nutty combination, making it a special treat.

# Columbus Day Cranberry Bread

*Ingredients:*

- 450 gr bread flour
- 240 ml warm water
- 2 teaspoons active dry yeast
- 50 gr sugar
- 1 teaspoon salt
- 150 gr dried cranberries

*Instructions:*

1. Add water, sugar, and yeast to the bread machine pan. Wait for 10 minutes.
2. Add flour, salt, and cranberries.
3. Set machine to basic bread setting.

*Tip:* This bread is slightly tangy due to the cranberries. It pairs well with turkey sandwiches.

## Arbor Day Nut Bread

*Ingredients:*

- 450 gr bread flour
- 240 ml warm water
- 2 teaspoons active dry yeast
- 50 gr brown sugar
- 1 teaspoon salt
- 100 gr mixed nuts (e.g., walnuts, pecans, almonds)

*Instructions:*

1. Add water, sugar, and yeast to the bread machine pan. Wait for 10 minutes.
2. Add flour, salt, and nuts.
3. Set machine to basic bread setting.

*Tip:* Celebrate trees with this nutty bread. It's crunchy and rich.

**General Tip for All Recipes:** Always measure ingredients accurately, and if possible, use a scale for the best results. Making bread is part art, part science, and the right proportions can make a big difference in the final product.

Made in United States
North Haven, CT
08 October 2023

42517125R00083